Common Sense Ideas
ON GROWING UP

A Teenager's Guide To Everyday Problems
A Parent's Guide To Understanding

Jan Keegan

Author's Tranquility Press
ATLANTA, GEORGIA

Copyright © 2024 by Jan Keegan

All rights reserved. No part of this publication may be reproduced, distributed or transmitted in any form or by any means, including photocopying, recording, or other electronic or mechanical methods, without the prior written permission of the publisher, except in the case of brief quotations embodied in critical reviews and certain other noncommercial uses permitted by copyright law. For permission requests, write to the publisher, addressed, "Attention: Permissions Coordinator," at the address below:

Jan Keegan/Author's Tranquility Press
3900 N Commerce Dr. Suite 300 #1255
Atlanta, GA 30344
www.authorstranquilitypress.com

Ordering Information:
Quantity sales. Special discounts are available on quantity purchases by corporations, associations, retail book sellers, and others. For details, contact the "Special Sales Department" at the address above.

Common Sense Ideas In Growing Up/ Jan Keegan

Art and Design Illustration by Heather H. Hatheway

Library of Congress Control Number: 2024921525

ISBN
Hardback: 978-1-965075-73-9
Paperback: 978-1-965075-27-2
eBook: 978-1-965075-28-9

TABLE OF CONTENTS

INTRODUCTION v

GROWING UP 1

PEER PRESSURE 5

PARENTAL AND FAMILY STRESS 9

DRUG AND ALCOHOL USAGE 13

PHYSICAL AND SEXUAL DEVELOPMENT 17

CAREER GOALS 21

SUMMARY 25

INTRODUCTION

Growing up is a hard and trying to experience that we must go through in order to achieve independence and self-responsibility. Because of the variety of experiences that we must go through to achieve emotional and physical maturity, we may, on occasion, incur several emotional feelings that leave us feeling alone and different from others. We might even question whether our thoughts and feelings that we are experiencing are normal or not.

In our discussion on growing up, we will first define what growing up is, and then discuss some of the factors that influence us during the growing up process. Hopefully, the insight provided by this discussion will help the young person realize that most of the feelings experienced while growing up are normal; and will enable him or her to better understand and adjust to the daily problems that occur in the process of growing up.

GROWING UP

Growing up is a process that occurs which causes us to grow toward independence and self-responsibility. The process causes our attitude to change from one of dependence on others to one of acceptance of responsibility for ourselves. The process usually occurs from the time we begin to think for ourselves (mid-school age) and continues over a period of time in which we begin to recognize and accept responsibility for ourselves (later adolescence-early adulthood). We can call ourselves grown-up when we can make a decision, and then accept the consequences of that decision, not blaming others for the results of the decision that we made. We can call ourselves grown-up when we can accept our mistakes and our successes; and in actuality, when we can accept ourselves for what we are, and continue to strive for ourselves and our goals.

Does the process of growing up have to be a distressing experience? No, not necessarily! However, few of us can complete the process of growing up without experiencing some anxiety and pain. How many times have we heard a well-meaning adult say, "Growing up hurts" or "Growing up is hard"? Because the process of growing up occurs over that period of time when we are young, when our experiences in socialization and problem-solving have been limited; and when our ideas and values have not been defined; perhaps these combined circumstances cause our growing up process to be painful.

During the process of growing up, we often find our thoughts and feelings to be confusing and conflicting. On the one hand, we do not want or need the advice or counsel of our loved ones. On the other hand, under the masks we sometimes wear, when a problem or a crisis does arise, we are secretly crying for help and guidance. How many times have we wished that someone was with us to help us face a major problem? Yet, when we are faced with a problem, we often find it hard to ask for help and support from our friends and loved ones. After all, we are trying to grow up and be independent! all, we are trying to grow up and be independent! So, at times, we find ourselves having conflicting thoughts that can add to the problems of growing up.

Any discussion on growing up must include the many fac tors that influence our day-to-day lives including peer pressure, parental and family stress, usage of drugs and alcohol, physical and sexual development, and career goals. Let's examine each of these factors so that we may gain some insight and understanding on how they affect us on a day- to-day basis while we are growing up.

COMMON SENSE IDEAS ON GROWING UP

PEER PRESSURE

Of all the influences that affect us while growing up, peer pressure has a very important effect on our daily decisions we make in our lives. Most of us recognize the importance of peer pressure in our lives; however, rarely do we stop and think about what peer pressure is and how it affects us.

Peer pressure is that pressure or influence exerted on us by our friends to help us conform to our friends' ideas and perceptions. There are two concepts we must consider when we are discussing peer pressure. One is the importance of being accepted by our friends; the other is the importance of not being different from our friends.

Why is being accepted by our friends so important to us when we are growing up? When we are young, we begin to develop our socialization skills and, in the process, we begin to become aware of our feelings about ourselves. By nature, we want to feel good and be comfortable with ourselves. When our actions and behavior are acceptable to our friends, we receive favorable reactions from our friends, which in turn makes us feel good about ourselves. On the other hand, when our behaviors or actions are such as not to be acceptable to our friends, we receive negative reactions from our friends that cause us to feel rejected and uncomfortable with ourselves. So we act and react to pressure from our friends to achieve good feelings and a positive image of ourselves.

Closely related to the concept of being accepted by our friends is the concept of not being different. To be different sets us apart from our friends and decreases the likelihood of being accepted by them. The reason the concept of not being different from our friends is important when discussing peer pressure is that by nature, most of us are different to a certain degree and we develop differently as we are growing up. Some differences that develop, such as good looks or physique, can help us establish ourselves among our friends. different sets us apart from our friends and decreases the likelihood of being accepted by them. The reason the concept of not being different from our friends is important when discussing peer pressure is that by nature, most of us are different to a certain degree and we develop differently as we are growing up. Some differences that develop, such as good looks or physique, can help us establish ourselves among our friends. However, some physical qualities that are different result in what we think will cause a negative reaction from our friends, thus reducing our good feelings about ourselves. For instance, being overweight, or developing a bad case of acne brings attention to us, thus increasing our self-consciousness of being different and perhaps not being accepted by our friends.

So we strive not to be different and to be accepted by our friends, and in the process, we succumb to peer pressure whether we are aware of it or not. Our decisions on how we dress, our choices of hair style, the clothes we wear, our decisions on our in-school subjects or out-of-school activities, are largely based on our need to be accepted by our friends. Because some of the decisions we make in growing up can have a life-long effect on us even though the decision itself may seem simple, we need to be aware of how much peer pressure influences us. Only as we begin to recognize peer pressure control on our lives, can we begin to define our own values and ideas in the growing up process.

COMMON SENSE IDEAS ON GROWING UP

PARENTAL AND FAMILY STRESS

Often in the process of growing up, we find ourselves in disagreement with our parents and other adults who have authority over us. These disagreements happen because in our quest for independence, we begin to think for ourselves and make our own decisions, which often conflict with those who have authority over us. This can lead to much stress and unhappiness in our family lives.

Other causes of stress and disruption in our family lives may be due to conditions beyond our control. Many of us may experience much unhappiness and loneliness as a result of our parents' difficulties in dealing with their day-to-day lives. There may be economic or job problems to deal with between our parents; maybe one parent lost a job or even with both parents working, they are having difficulties in making ends meet. Whatever the situation, at times the stress or anxiety level at home may be high.

When we sense increased stress in our family lives as we are growing up, we often feel rejected, unhappy, alone. Whereas in the past, we felt happy and safe in our relationships with our parents, we now may be realizing that these relationships are changing, and perhaps even breaking down. We may feel guilty in imposing our own difficulties and problems on our parents when they themselves are having difficulties in handling their own problems. Or, we may choose to believe that our parents don't care about us because they are involved with their own problems. problems. Or, we may choose to believe that our parents don't care about us because they are involved with their own problems.

When we are faced with family and parental stress while growing up, we must try to deal with our feelings. Being able to talk to someone often helps us to sort our feelings and place them into perspective. There are other important people in our lives, whether a good friend, a grandparent, a Sunday School teacher or a school counselor, that we have previously developed

a relationship with, who care about us and our feelings. We might have to seek someone to help us, but there is someone who can help us.

We should be aware when we are experiencing loneliness and despair over family problems, that we are not the only person in the world with family or parental stress. Often, it helps us to know that others may have similar problems to ours and are trying to deal with them as we are.

During the process of dealing with the problems that family stress can cause, we must remember to have some understanding of our parents. Most of our parents love us very much. They have often got caught up in a very complex society in their efforts to provide for us. They too, may suffer from discouragement and uncertainty at times. By being able to share an understanding with our parents, we may be able to deal with our own feelings better and decrease the stress in our families.

COMMON SENSE IDEAS ON GROWING UP

DRUG AND ALCOHOL USAGE

If we continue our common-sense approach in discussing factors that influence us in the process of growing up, we might approach the subject of drug and alcohol usage by discussing the bad effects of drugs and alcohol on our physical, social, and mental beings. However, in reality, while growing up, we do not like to be told, and in fact deny the bad effects of drug or alcohol usage on us. The fact that we don't like to take advice not only about drugs and alcohol usage, but other issues as well, from our parents and other adults when growing up can be attributed to certain rebellious attitudes that are necessary in our efforts to gain independence; for it is by rebelling against our parents and other adults that we begin to make decisions and actually grow toward maturity. So with this in mind, let's put forth a few common-sense ideas about drug and alcohol usage that can be examined from an objective standpoint.

The first idea that we will examine is the idea that in some cases drug and, or alcohol usage leads to abuse. There is a tendency among some of us that the more we use drugs or alcohol, the more we will want to use them. So we establish a pattern in our lives, an arrangement in our daily life styles, so that we might use and abuse drugs or alcohol. The desire for these substances begins to control our lives, the decisions we make, who our friends are, where we hang out, and so on. The control over our lives by these substances is often insidious, in that full, or almost full control over our lives has occurred slowly, on a day-to-day basis, and we don't realize what is happening to us.

The second idea that we need to examine is that the actual results of drug and alcohol usage and abuse lead to a lack of control of one's thought processes, thus reducing our judgmental abilities. Getting bombed may seem to be fun, and even recognizing ourselves as being out of control, may accentuate what seems to be fun; but more often than not, this lack of control causes us to do things we would not ordinarily do, often causing damages that reach far beyond our most imaginative conceptions.

The third and last idea to be examined is how the after effects of drug or alcohol usage affect our daily lives. Irritability, nervousness, headaches, and stomach cramps are just a few of the after effects of drug and alcohol abuse. These effects are bound to affect us in our relationships with others, in our school work, in our day-to-day lives. Problems that normally occur in our lives are compounded by our irritability and nervousness. Decisions, no matter how unimportant they may seem, are made and can be influenced by our irritability that is present because of drug or alcohol abuse.

So if we consider how easily drug or alcohol usage can gain control over our lives, causing problems with loss of judgment and interference with our normal problem-solving techniques and decision-making abilities; maybe we can apply maybe we can apply some common-sense ideas that will influence our decisions on using alcohol or drugs in our lives.

COMMON SENSE IDEAS ON GROWING UP

PHYSICAL AND SEXUAL DEVELOPMENT

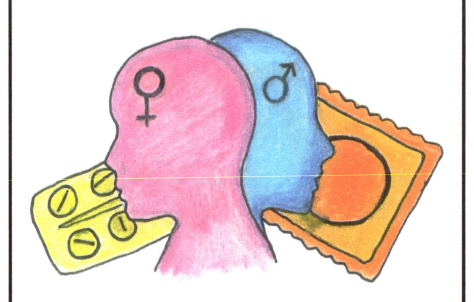

As if the process of growing up is not complicated enough by the influences we have discussed, the process of physical developing into young men and young women occurs during the same time period that we are growing toward emotional maturity. Physical development in itself, being a normal process, should not cause us too many problems if we understand that in time, we will grow to the potential of our genetic make-up. What is important about physical development is that as we are all growing at different rates, we might find ourselves in the predicament of being quite different from our peers. For instance, we might be the shortest or the tallest among our peers which can cause us to develop a feeling of increased anxiety and self-conscious ness that can influence our sense of well-being.

During the process of developing physically, our bodies are releasing hormones that are necessary in directing our bodies' physical growth. These fluctuating levels of hormones can cause us to react to our environment in a sporadic manner. For instance, we might react to a comic situation by laughing too loudly; then, when realizing we are drawing attention to ourselves, we suddenly become embarrassed and withdraw from the situation. Or we might find that one minute we are happy to the point of giggling; and the next minute find ourselves crying over nothing. Even though this fluctuation of emotions is a normal process, eventually as our bodies' hormone levels stabilize, and as we increase our socialization skills; we find we are able to handle our reactions to our environment in a more stable manner; and thus increase our good feelings of ourselves.

Correlating with physical development of our bodies is our sexual development. By the time most of us have reached our mid-teens, we have gone through puberty. Puberty has been defined as that time that our bodies' sexual organs have developed to the point that reproduction can take place. The development of our reproductive organs takes place over a period of time and as in physical development, will differ with each of us. Along with the development of our reproductive organs are changes that occur to the rest of our bodies. For instance, voice changes and increased facial, axillary, and pubic hair occur in boys. Girls develop increased axillary and pubic hair as well as increased size in breasts and the development of the menstrual cycle.

With all of these physical and sexual changes going on with us during our growing up years, we can become con fused and unsure of ourselves, particularly if we don't view these changes as a normal process of growing toward physical maturity. We may even develop feelings of self-consciousness or even embarrassment about the changes that are occurring to our bodies. During these times of experiencing mixed-up emotions, we need to keep in mind that our bodes' development is undergoing a normal process, and what we experience emotionally as a result of these physical and sexual changes, is normal. In time, as we adjust to these changes, these feelings of awkwardness, self-consciousness, or embarrassment, will occur less often because we can accept these changes as a necessary part of growing up.

COMMON SENSE IDEAS ON GROWING UP

CAREER GOALS

As we have seen in our discussion of growing up, the process of growing toward maturity and independence can be a chaotic and sometimes trying experience. Our reactions of dealing with our everyday problems are influenced by our peers, our parents, our physical and sexual growth, and fluctuating emotions. As if we didn't have enough pressure exerted on us, we are constantly being bombarded with questions and ideas concerning what we are going to do with our futures. Should we go to college to further our education, or should we develop a skill by going to trade school? Maybe we should just get a job and forget about furthering our education. Whatever our decision is concerning our future, there are a few common-sense ideas that might help us in making some of the decisions about our future and our career choices.

For instance, each of us has a special ability or aptitude to accomplish something very good. Some of us can work with people very well; others of us have a special talent, such as being able to draw or build objects. Some of us are very good in math; other of us have a good aptitude for science. Whatever our abilities and talents are, we need to stop on occasion and analyze what we are good at. Once we recognize what our abilities and interests are, then we can make choices in our daily lives, such as choosing some of our school subjects or the type of after-school jobs we might take; that will give us more experience and direction toward our future careers.

Another common-sense idea relating to our future goals is to make a plan as to how to achieve what we are aspiring to. Most of us have dreams and ideas as to what we want to do and what we want for ourselves in the future. However, unless we develop a plan as to how to achieve what we want for our futures, we will most likely find ourselves haphazardly going through life and later realizing that we have strayed far from what our goals and dreams were at an earlier age.

To develop a plan to achieve our goals for the future, one must consider what resources are available for guidance and help. For instance, a career or guidance counselor at school may be an extremely helpful resource in helping one make present decisions that will affect future goals. Other resources available include our parents and other role models that can offer advice and guidance that can help us form a plan for our future goals. However, our best resource will be ourselves and how we use our knowledge and abilities to accomplish what we want to with our lives. Being able to recognize ourselves and our abilities and qualities is an asset in itself and will correlate with other resources to help us make decisions regarding our future goals.

COMMON SENSE IDEAS ON GROWING UP

SUMMARY

As we have seen in our discussion on growing up, the process of growing toward emotional maturity can be a painful and trying experience. Because of the variety of influences and other factors that we encounter in the process of growing up, we may, at times, have feelings of loneliness, despair, confusion, embarrassment, and awkwardness; which can lead to much unhappiness for us. Understanding ourselves better and understanding the factors that influence our day-to-day lives can help us adjust to our problems and perhaps prevent future unhappiness for us. As long as we can relate our feelings to others in similar circumstances and realize that what we experience while growing up is normal, some of these emotional feelings will decrease in intensity; thus helping us to feel better about ourselves and increasing our sense of well-being.

COMMON SENSE IDEAS ON GROWING UP

Milton Keynes UK
Ingram Content Group UK Ltd.
UKHW020135021224
451809UK00020B/269